Worker Learning and Worktime Flexibility

Gretl S. Meier

A Policy Discussion Paper

Library of Congress Cataloging in Publication Data

Meier, Gretl S.
  Worker learning and worktime flexibility.

  Includes bibliographical references.
  1. Hours of labor—United States.   Women—Employ-
ment—United States.   3. Occupational training for women
—United States.   4. Employees, Training of—United
States.   I. Title.
HD6066.U5M45   1983   331.4'2592'0973   83-1348
ISBN 0-88099-007-4 (pbk.)

The Author

Gretl S. Meier is a graduate of Mount Holyoke College (B.A., Political Science), Radcliffe College of Harvard University (M.A., American History), and did further graduate work in International Relations at L'Institute d'Etudes Politiques of the University of Paris. She has been co-director of New Ways to Work, a San Francisco-Palo Alto employment resource agency, a research assistant at The Brookings Institution, a staff member of the first Mayor's Commission on Puerto Rican Affairs in New York City, and a consultant to the Human Relations Office of the New Haven Unified School District in Union City, California.

Ms. Meier is the author of *Job Sharing: A New Pattern for Quality of Work and Life* and *Job Sharing in the Schools,* as well as numerous general articles on job sharing, and a contributor to *New Work Patterns* by Stanley D. Nollen. She co-authored the final report of the CETA-sponsored Job Sharing Project of New Ways to Work, and testified in 1976 before the U.S. Senate Subcommittee on Employment, Poverty, and Migratory Labor on the need for alternative work patterns. She has also been concerned with European experiences with work flexibility and their relevance to alternative work patterns in the U.S. In 1978, under a grant from the German Marshall Fund, she represented New Ways to Work at meetings with European colleagues to explore these issues.

Preface

This study explores the feasibility of research on how flexible work patterns might extend education and training opportunities. Although its findings are relevant to a wider employee population, this preliminary inquiry has concentrated on the combined impact of flexible worktime and training policies on women in low status jobs.

The underlying problem is that, although women are entering and remaining in the labor force in the U.S. at an unprecedented rate, 80 percent are still confined to the low skilled jobs in clerical, sales, operative, craft and service occupations. Many, without access to higher education before entering employment, are still unable to take advantage of employer-sponsored learning activities. In contrast to managers and professionals who participate in education and training programs in disproportionately high numbers, these workers are often barred by the more rigid scheduling of their work hours.

A partial solution to the inequity in access to learning opportunities may lie in the applicability of flexible work patterns: flextime, the compressed workweek, permanent part time, and job sharing. Might these women utilize new scheduling to better balance work and their primary home responsibilities and, *at the same time,* to take greater advantage of education and training in order to renew themselves and to find better jobs and new occupations?

The findings of this report are based on a review of related literature and, more specifically, on a series of informal interviews and preliminary data collected at selected work sites during 1981. To identify the potential gains of the relationship between flexible work patterns and learning opportunities as well as the problems that must be overcome, the sample included companies with broad participation in training and education programs as well as firms offering new work schedules. These discussions have revealed the nature and range of additional data that would be required for more substantive study. Equally important, they have made a start at raising management interest in linking two areas of personnel policy which, until now, have been quite separate.

Education, training and retraining requirements pose an alarming national problem—not only because of the current high levels of recession-induced unemployment, but also for reasons of structural change. Structural transformations in the economy—as old jobs obsolesce and new jobs occur in the technical and service sectors—require a repatterning of labor force skills. Moreover, the changing nature of job supply and diminished internal mobility will harshly affect women and other minorities, especially if enforcement of affirmative action guidelines weakens.

Employer-sponsored learning, often termed "the shadow system of education," its extent and equity of access, will be subjected to greater pressures as the public sector role diminishes. Reduced federal expenditures for training, the new federalism, and government overtures for an expanded private sector role will strain employer-sponsored schemes already in place. And although their long-range implications cannot yet be fully analyzed, the cuts in government aid to education will limit the development of the human capital required for industry and business needs in the not-too-distant future.

Despite its focus on employer-sponsored activities, this paper presumes that occupational orientation and re-orientation are but one part of worker learning. The other, reflecting individual human values, depends on a more broadly based content that aims to fulfill personal potential, off and on the job. The fusion of practical and theoretical knowledge has become even more critical as all Americans have been forced to adjust to the often overwhelming pace of social and political as well as economic change. Such learning can make "... a determinative difference between a reprieve of opportunity and a lifetime sentence to frustration, and obsolescence."[1]

Learning is addictive. The line between education and training may be blurred when the latter moves beyond specific tasks to adaptable skills and provides the basis for the new common literacy in language and numbers. Instruction which takes place to enhance *work* rather than narrow *job related* skills may often encourage further learning. If new means can be found to promote the availability of broader training, then the longer-range educational goal may also be better served.

This report is intended to provide a basis for a more informed discussion of the policy questions, rather than to serve as a proposal for specific subsequent research. To this end, Part I first sets forth the "Perspectives:" the trends that may influence the use of flexible patterns and the provision of educational and training opportunities. It then reviews the practice of new work patterns and of employer-sponsored learning activities. Part II discusses some examples of "Recent Experience," suggesting the types of data needed for more complete examination, but focusing on the necessary conditions to establish the relationship. Part III, "Future Research: Some Considerations," outline the principal research issues which have emerged during this exploratory study. The report concludes with a brief discussion of policy for employers.

I am grateful to The Carnegie Corporation of New York and to Barbara D. Finberg, vice-president for Program and Program Officer, for encouraging the initiation of this study and for the financial assistance that made it possible. I am also indebted to the W. E. Upjohn Institute and to the late E. Earl Wright, its director, for additional support and for the opportunity to publish this paper.

In the preparation of this study, a large number of individuals have generously shared their research and helped with advice. I especially wish to thank Paul E. Barton of the National Institute for Work and Learning, Nevser Stacy of the National Institute of Education and Janice N. Hedges, formerly of the Bureau of Labor Statistics. Above all, I am indebted to the managers and other employees of the 24 companies who provided data and other technical information. Although I have benefitted from these individuals in official and unofficial capacities, I am, of course, solely responsible for the conclusions of this study and for any errors of judgment or fact which it contains.

NOTE

1. Willard Wirtz, "Foreword," in Paul E. Barton, *Worklife Transitions* (New York, NY: McGraw-Hill Book Company, 1982), pp. vii.

Contents

I. PERSPECTIVES

Changes Affecting Workplaces and Worker Needs

Economic and social trends projected for the coming decade are likely to focus continuing attention on the need to develop the skills and maintain the morale of American workers. Concern over declining productivity, together with demographic shifts and workers' changing values, all suggest the importance of developing more effective opportunities for education and training and for expanding the use of flexible work patterns.

Declining productivity is already causing a search for ways to improve workers' performance. Although few employers look to flexible schedules as part of the solution, many are discovering that the introduction of new work patterns--with its resultant higher employee morale and more effective use of time--often contributes to increased productivity. More important, even though conclusive empirical evidence of links to productivity is lacking, employers have been investing increasingly larger sums in education and training. The pressure for a more rapid application of new technology will now call for expanded retraining of workers: those who will be forced to switch occupations, others whose skill requirements may be increased in low level jobs, and still others whose new jobs will require greater technological knowledge.

Productivity concerns are also affecting changes in management styles, particularly in medium and large sized firms. The development of new horizontal as well as vertical relationships, through "matrix" management, enhances the responsibility for organizational effectiveness of

all supervisors and managers. It has strongly
influenced the nature of corporate education and
training. 1/ It may, in the future, also
contribute to further consideration of the need
for and the means to promote performance of all
employees. In some U.S. firms, although far less
than in other industrialized countries, added
awareness of education and training deficiencies
arises with moves to enhance worker participation
in organizational problemsolving and
decisionmaking. Other efforts in job redesign
require re-examination of task analysis and better
worker preparation for these redefined
responsbilities. They may often call attention to
changing the scheduling of work so that jobs may
be more productive and more satisfying.

New management styles are emerging also to
meet changing worker values. A more widespread
recognition of "quality-of-worklife" issues has
come about in part because of the slow but steady
decline in job satisfaction. 2/ Because a
workforce with generally higher than ever
education credentials is dissatisfied with
routinized jobs, it is seeking more varied job
content. Some employees are asking, too, for
better control over their worktime. Men as well
as women are looking to balance work with other
aspects of their daily and lifetime family and
leisure needs. As many more adults participate in
informal and formal schooling, an increasing
number are questioning the traditional life-cycle
stages of education-work-retirement.

Demographic changes will further affect these
issues as a more heterogeneous population is
expected to include larger numbers of men and
women with a lowered likelihood of job mobility.
3/ The coming decade will see a proportionately
larger number of older workers as the age of the

working population rises with a decline of the post-war "baby boom." This increase in the number of prime age workers with a higher level of educational attainment than before suggests that opportunities to advance in organizations may be less than worker expectations. Education and training will assume more importance as one of the several means to achieve horizontal as well as vertical mobility. Furthermore, older people, who will become a large proportion of the population, are likely to be working longer, a result of inflationary pressures and of the extended mandatory retirement age (raised to 70 in the private sector and eliminated in the public sector by the 1978 Age Discrimination Act Amendments). Many older workers may be forced to prepare for second and third careers, often through jobs which are more flexibly scheduled.

The expected rise in the numbers of poorly skilled, non-English speaking workers will also pose a significant challenge to industry and business. It will tend to exacerbate the problem already disturbing employers, as many high school graduates now appear to lack basic skills in math and English. At a time when a minimum of college education or other "credentialing" has become the prerequisite for a variety of blue-collar as well as white-collar jobs in the expanding service and information sectors, the lack of skill development in workers disadvantaged at an early age is likely to become even more acute.

Of primary importance, however, for the purposes of this paper, will be the issues arising from the "feminization of the labor market"--the expected continued increase in the proportion of workers who are women. 4/ About 52 million women, it is anticipated, will be in the labor force by 1990, an increase of about one million a year.

Nearly all of the projected additions will be aged 25-54, most will be married, and the majority will have minor children. The growing prevalence of two-earner married couples together with the anticipated high number of parents who are single (even for some period of time) will undoubtedly bring to the forefront the search for new means to achieve family well-being and expand the demand for jobs which permit a better balance between home and work. Also strongly implied is a more critical role for education and training as women seek preparation to: 1) make transitions from home to school, 2) advance to higher job levels within traditionally female occupations and, 3) surmount the barriers which now make difficult their entry and promotion in the predominately male professions.

The overriding question raised by the increased labor force participation of women will be <u>whether greater vertical and occupational mobility can be achieved</u>. Otherwise, the added numbers of women seeking employment will serve only to sharpen the competition for the same low paying jobs in traditionally female occupations which the great majority of women workers now hold. Indeed, because women are still entering stereotypically female, low level positions, according to some observers, the rise to date of women's participation cannot be considered a sign of true progress. Instead, they contend, the result has been a larger proportion than before of women employed at or near entry level. <u>5</u>/

A Conference Board report on the advances in women's employment opportunities from 1970-1975 points out that change is underway, but cautions that the process is complex, particularly in male-intensive industries where resistance has been great. <u>6</u>/ It found that, even in

white-collar work where women hold more highly
paid jobs, major progress has been made only in
those industries with traditionally larger female
workforces--banking, insurance, retailing and
communications. The real problem again is that,
unless provision is made for upward mobility, when
women do move into nontraditional fields they tend
to remain at entry level and continue to be
segregated.

This study on the feasibility of new work
patterns to increase participation in education
and training activities does not presume
that the availability and utilization
of such opportunities, alone, will lead to
greater upward and cross-occupational mobility.
Antidiscrimination laws and regulations are of
primary importance; even though they best
redistribute employment opportunities when the
total number of jobs available is growing.
Internal mobility is, of course, also affected by
equitable promotion policies and other procedures
such as job-posting. Additionally, career
counseling and informal on-the-job training, which
includes the team skills traditionally available
to male employees, will make formal education and
training programs more effective opportunities.
Other supports, above all, perhaps, the provision
of child care, will facilitate the career mobility
of working women. But, although education and
training have had a lower return for women than
men, (i.e., women of similar educational
attainment to men generally have had much lower
job status), these activities still carry
significant economic value. 7/ If new jobs of the
future are to be sex-neutral, new initiatives in
training and education will be essential.

In sum, attention to both worker education and
training and to flexible time schedules will be

heightened during the coming decade. However, it is of crucial importance that future consideration also be directed to changing existing patterns in each of these areas of personnel policy. In order for new schedules to offer more than a temporary palliative as an accommodation to some working women, they must also begin to better fulfill their more long-range potential to expand new job levels and occupations for women as a group. Otherwise, a real danger exists that flexible hours may, paradoxically, reinforce the same narrow occupational stereotyping of women.

Moreover, if continuous learning activities are to be opened to the great majority of employed women who are now outside the structure of opportunity, participation must be encouraged by supportive policies, including the use of flexible hours. Although these two concerns have, until now, appeared to be quite separate, policymakers might now begin to consider whether and by what means they might be advantageously linked.

Investigation of each of these topics in the last decade has yielded substantial data through numerous surveys and case studies. Despite the fact that neither learning activities nor new worktime practice lends itself to generalization because each is diverse and often informal in nature, the brief overview which follows may usefully serve as background to some specific current experience of their linkage.

New Work Patterns: Possibilities and Problems

Flextime
New work patterns--flextime, the compressed workweek and permanent part time--are in greater use by American workers than is generally realized. About one-fifth of the workers in the

U.S. are not working a traditional 40-hour, 5-day schedule. Of these, 7.6 million workers or 12 percent of those in full-time, non-farm, wage and salary jobs are on flexible schedules. 8/ The unique nature of this pattern has been aptly described as a transfer of some control over the timing of work from supervisors to individual workers, even though it does not change total hours. 9/

Flextime is particularly promising because it offers the kind of "free" time which might be used easily for education and training--a regular daily open time at the beginning and end of the working day. Moreover, several types of flextime are possible: (1) those within the 8-hour day requiring starting and quitting time either within a specific or variable period, and (2) others where credit and debit hours are allowed as long as the total hours worked fulfill weekly or monthly organizational requirements, or where core time is required only on certain days.

It is important, however, to remember that the degree of flexibility open to and chosen by workers varies considerably even within an organization, at the same site or from one location to another. According to a recent estimate, about 20 percent of organizations used flextime for at least some of their employees in 1980. 10/

Women workers are less likely than men to be working in flextime schedules (as are young workers and union members). Data on occupational categories shows a widespread use by sales personnel, managers and administrators, professionals and technicians. Practice in these occupations is generally long standing and informal. Although relatively lower, the use of flextime by clerical and service workers is substantial (9.8 percent and 8.7 percent of the total number on flexible schedules), representing a recent development in which eligibility and schedule rules are more carefully prescribed. Female-intensive industries are also high users--finance and insurance (with real estate), second only to the federal government.

Both employers and employees have found positive results from the introduction of flextime. Workers value easier commuting and the reduction of the pressure to be at work at a fixed time. They find flextime helps to balance their need for both free time and time for family responsibilities. Despite some problems of equity in eligibility and of initial supervisor resistance, employers generally cite these overriding benefits to employees as their rationale for adopting flextime. Several studies show economic results favorable to the organization. As is true of other alternative patterns, however, the initial decisions to implement tend to be based on the need to solve particular business problems (tardiness, absenteeism) or to reflect the belief of senior management that flextime is the "right thing to do," rather than on careful economic analyses.

Compressed Schedules

Current use of compressed schedules would seem to offer a much narrower but still possible linkage with education and training opportunities. The actual hours of nonworktime are usually more limited--from a half day to two full days weekly, depending on whether the 3, 4 or 4-1/2 day schedule is used. Furthermore, in comparison with flextime, use of compressed schedules is low (2.7 million as of May 1980) and numbers have edged up only slightly since the early 1970s. 11/

Use of this time pattern may remain comparatively restricted because advantages and disadvantages cannot be easily generalized; compressed schedules are particularly firm- and occupation-specific. They have been primarily used: (1) in manufacturing for shift work and for 24-hour, 7-day week continuous-process industries where start-ups and shut-downs are costly; (2) where capital equipment may be underutilized; and (3) where work is located at a considerable distance from workers' homes (as protective service jobs). But such schedules can also cause organizational problems because of the difficulty of synchronizing operations within and between firms. Use of compressed schedules is also limited (as is the flextime credit and debit scheme) by conflicting union contracts and legislation on overtime premiums. Workers have found that although the compressed week gives a longer block of free time and reduces the number of commuting trips, it may also complicate social and home life, particularly for families with young children.

It may be somewhat surprising that, for industry as a whole, recent data reveal that, almost as many women as men are working in compressed schedules. In terms of occupations, clerical workers are less likely to use a shortened week than are employees in other occupations, but we might assume that many women are included in the high use occupations of service and factory operatives. Shortened workweeks are relatively rare in female-intensive industries (among the lowest users are finance, insurance and real estate) compared with local public administration (including police and fire personnel). The small proportion of clerical workers who are on such schedules may however, be employed in insurance and banking. 12/

Part Time: Its Several Variations

Part-time employment would seem to offer a natural linkage with education and training. Generally defined as work of less than 35 hours a week, part-time jobs have traditionally afforded a means for younger adults to support their continued learning. Part-time work has grown rapidly over the past 20 years, from about 1 in 12 workers to 1 in 7, and now appears to remain steady. Part timers are employed in more than one-half of all firms, although they account for usually only 2 to 7 percent of each firm's workforce. 13/ Furthermore, many employers are now regularizing the new status of these employees, differentiating among them by categories which range in title from "supplementals" to "prime-time" workers. Some companies offer salaries and fringe benefits comparable to those accorded full-time workers in similar jobs; only a few have expanded the occupational range open to part-time employment or have extended promotion opportunities to part-time employees. Whether the pattern can now be used in a broader fashion so as to encourage education and training for prime-age workers, particularly women, depends in large measure on the success of current efforts to promote such changes.

These initiatives to develop part-time employment as a longer term, career work pattern rather than a temporary, peripheral arrangement, however, must first counter the long prevailing practices and perceptions of part-time workers. Women, and the young and old, who are considered to have little sense of job attachment, are those who traditionally work part time. Although not all part timers are confined to the unskilled labor market, most are concentrated in the trade and service industries where uneven scheduling demands make their employment most attractive to employers. Because these jobs often involve discrete tasks or workloads with predictable cycles, employers have been able to meet special operating problems by increasing shifts. Sales, clerical and service workers and laborers are likely to work less than full time more often than managers, supervisors or skilled craft workers who find few part-time positions because of organizational perceptions of high skill requirements, continuous work flow and the need for communication.

Part-time work has generally yielded significant economic returns to employers. Superior job performance by part timers often reduces labor costs, as does the lack of many or all of the fringe benefits accorded to full-time workers. Part timers are frequently paid less than full-time employees, but the wage differential may be largely due to the fact that part time is still confined to lower level jobs for men as well as women. 14/

Given these considerations, part-time employees and their employers have rarely invested in education and training. Workers, both male and female, on part-time schedules theoretically have more nonwork time for training and education, but realistically have far less incentive when the availability of higher level jobs on a part-time basis is low. Nor are they as likely as full timers to be able to afford the cost of education and training. Employers traditionally have been reluctant to train even those women who work full time, generally citing higher turnover and absentee rates. According to some studies, turnover and absenteeism often show a greater correlation to low job status, lack of advancement and other factors than to gender alone. 15/

The more recent development of <u>career</u> <u>oriented</u> or <u>permanent</u> <u>part-time</u> <u>employment</u> may well encourage greater provision of opportunities and more widespread participation in education and training activities. Beyond the regularity of hours available for learning, incentive is enhanced when such jobs, considered permanent by the organization, offer advancement possibilities and a range of fringe benefits comparable to those accorded full-time employees. Although occupational segregation largely dominates, more regularized part-time employment has opened in jobs at higher skill levels and also in technical, professional and even managerial fields where continuous learning is a more accepted requirement for successful job performance.

In creating a greater number of permanent part-time positions in the last decade, employers have responded to the demands of an increasing number of workers--particularly women who wish to <u>remain</u> <u>in</u> as well as enter or re-enter the labor force. But, industry and business have also found that advantages frequently outweigh the added financial costs of social security and of fringe benefits, especially when the latter can be prorated or offered in cafeteria style. <u>16/</u> Aside from solving peak demand problems, companies have experienced reduced labor costs, including less overtime, as a result of a better match between work load and labor input. Many employers have maintained, if not improved, productivity due to improved employee morale and lower absenteeism and tardiness when employees are better able to organize nonwork activities outside of paid hours. Others report easier recruitment and, even more highly valued, a higher retention rate of skilled employees--those in mid-career or pre-retirement periods who wish to reduce hours for family, health and other reasons. In the case of skilled employees and in others where training involves future full-time workers, overall   hiring and training costs may actually be lowered.

Job Sharing

Job sharing,   which emerged in the late 1970s, combines some of the advantages of part-time with those of full-time employment.   The job is a regular full-time position but the jobholders work part time and divide salary and fringe benefits. This pattern may offer a unique potential for education and training in two respects.   Sharing allows a regular block of nonwork time, as do other part-time arrangements,   but because it affords greater continuity of coverage and, often, a combination of diverse skills, the new pattern may further expand the variety of occupations and levels of part-time jobs.   Furthermore, this form of flexibility may encourage a new type of on-the-job training whereby a partner with more highly developed skills may be teamed with a less experienced worker.

Unlike other new work patterns, no aggregate data exist on the extent of the usage of job sharing. Practice is sporadic in the private and in the public sector, although it has been more visibly utilized in the latter where educational institutions and local state agencies have offered job sharing along with other voluntary time reductions.   Current use by private organizations may well be greater than has been reported.   But, in general, it may be safely assumed that most of these employers have yet to expand job sharing beyond a proportionately few ad hoc arrangements in each organization. Occupations are thought to be diverse and job levels vary from professional to unskilled workers. An informal national survey in 1979 found that the largest percentage were teachers (26 percent) and administrators, coordinators/program developers (25 percent). 17/ A more recent Conference Board survey found that banking and insurance were the most likely of the industry users. 18/

Most job sharers, who are married women and are likely to have children at home, particularly value the ability to balance home and work. But, beyond this, they have often been able to find employment with salary and fringe benefits which are not generally available on a part-time, one person basis. In addition, some sharers find special advantage in supportive team collaboration and in the ability to trade time and tasks with a partner.

Employers have realized benefits from the use of job sharing similar to those discussed earlier of other part-time schedules. But, additionally, they report unique advantages of this pattern which can alleviate or solve many of the difficulties associated with part-time work. Greater flexibility is made possible when one employee covers for the other or when both partners adjust worktime to peak and slow periods. Furthermore, job sharing in professional and supervisory positions has often been found to bring a more productive performance than would a single full-time employee. The pattern has been especially successful in those higher level positions which require: (1) liaison within and outside the organization, (2) field work in different geographic locations and, (3) time pressures over long or short periods. 19/

The complications of instituting and managing job sharing which employers usually anticipate have been handled successfully in both the private and public sectors. Careful brokering to ensure complementarity between partners and between partners and the job, appropriate scheduling, and communication between sharers, co-workers and managers are all important conditions. And although this form of part-time employment requires, too, that employers revise policies on fringe benefits, many have instituted a system of prorating. Finally, in some instances, the inclusion of these and other provisions of parity with full timers has mitigated the union objections to even this form of part-time employment.

However, it must be pointed out that organized labor generally continues to object to the expansion of all part-time employment on the grounds that it will increase job competition, worsen unemployment and detract from the goals of shorter worktime for all workers. National leaders also contend that part-time jobs tend to downgrade occupational status, aid those workers less in need, and make future organizing difficult. This claim continues, despite the fact that at several local levels, union officers, recognizing the need to respond to workers' genuine desires for reduced hours, have negotiated for part-time options. They have acknowledged, in the bargaining process, that some jobs are more conducive to part-time hours and that the option of reducing worktime is often preferable as a temporary alternative to lay-offs.

Employer-Sponsored Education and Training

Unlike new work patterns which appear as a mutually advantageous accommodation with relatively few organizational costs or changes in structure, industry-sponsored education and training have become an expensive and complicated business necessity. 20/ It serves basically to adapt previously acquired skills and knowledge to the needs of the job. Increasingly, these activities also serve to compensate for deficiencies of general or vocational knowledge. They often include general knowledge designed to

enhance skills and to adapt to new technology.
This continuous learning takes place in both
informal on-the-job training by co-workers or
supervisors and through more formal instruction at
the worksite and elsewhere.

Although industry activities are still largely
considered a private affair, they have become of
greater public concern as billions of dollars are
spent and millions of Americans involved, and as
the desired effects on productivity and workers'
income and occupational mobility are questioned.
Yet, there are real difficulties in appraising
these diverse and often informal learning
activities. National surveys of
industry-sponsored education have been infrequent
and irregular. More important, they cannot
measure the unrecorded on-the-job activities which
are the most prevalent type of education and
training. And, despite the fact that the training
itself is becoming an industry, there has been
little examination of the total job to determine
the optimum relationship between activities which
take place on and off the job. 21/

Available information on the scope and nature
of employer-sponsored programs underlines the
uneven access to training. A 1980 review of the
diverse surveys concluded that:

--Employers provide formal education
opportunities in fewer than half of all firms, but
by more than 4 out of 5 of the larger firms;
--Among those larger firms, about 1 in 5 workers
takes part in training programs during any one
year, whereas the proportion is much smaller for
all industry;
--Management and white-collar workers, far more
than manual workers, are likely to participate in
formal training;

--Skill training accounts for only a small part
compared with learning about company products,
orientation and safety;
--Most companies which offer training do so on
company time. 22/

Occupation and industry also determine what
opportunities are available. The number and type
of opportunities vary significantly among
managerial employees, sales, supervisory
personnel, draft and operative workers, clerical
workers, and professional and technical workers.
The structure and technology of industries affects
the provision of education and training; high
technology employers, for example, find difficulty
in hiring already trained workers in most
occupations, depending on the location and
available labor supply.

The most specific data on the learning
opportunities available to nonexempt workers is
found in a 1981 Conference Board report of small,
medium and large size establishments in banking,
manufacturing, utilities and insurance. About 84
percent of the respondents provide on-site
education and training for both office and
clerical workers and production operations
workers. Banking, utilities and insurance,
particularly, provide programs for clerical and
office workers. Utilities and manufacturing
industries (to a somewhat lesser extent) offer
these activities to production and operations
workers. At the non-exempt level, training aims
largely at providing specific job skills or safety
and industrial skills to newly hired employees, in
contrast to training for lower level exempt
employees which aims to improve performance and to
prepare employees for new duties. 23/

Utilization of Tuition Assistance

The availability of tuition assistance programs, it might be assumed, would provide learning opportunities for low status workers. These are programs by which companies offer financial assistance to some or all employees to encourage them to study, generally at outside educational institutions. But the problem arises not in provision by employers but in utilization by workers.

The Conference Board survey referred to above found that tuition assistance is provided to full-time, white-collar workers, both exempt and nonexempt, by 90 percent of the companies surveyed. For blue-collar, nonexempt workers, tuition was provided by 80 percent of the companies. A 1977 study by the National Institute of Work and Learning estimated the number of workers eligible through union-employer negotiated plans as nearly 2 million. Participation, however, in all plans in the United States is generally considered at between 4 and 6 percent. Those most likely to utilize tuition aid are workers who already have a greater number of years of schooling and are in higher paid jobs--essentially white male workers. 24/

A study focusing on the utilization of tuition assistance by women found that lower participation related basically to women's position in low-status jobs. Although women of all income, education and skill levels took advantage of tuition assistance than did men at the same level, within either sex the status/hierarchy distinctions held true. Among the program-related barriers faced by women were the requirements that courses be job-related and tuition be paid in advance. Women were more likely than men to believe that education would not help on the job and to cite their "fear of returning to school." They were also more inclined to feel that "fatigue" and rigid work schedules barred their participation. 25/

Research on programs where tuition aid is highly used by employees at all job levels has found that organizations develop specific means to encourage employee participation when they are committed to broadly-based education and training programs. Where this kind of commitment exists, opportunities for nonexempt workers and women among them are made more effective. In order to assess the relative value of new work patterns to increase participation in education and training, this preliminary study will take into account the ways in which worktime is adjusted in some of these organizations.

NOTES

1. Ernest A. Lynton, The Role of Colleges and Universities in Corporate Education. Draft Manuscript, Center for Studies in Policy and the Public Interest, University of Massachusetts, 1981, p. 3.

2. See, for example, Robert P. Quinn and Graham L. Staines, The 1977 Quality of Employment Survey: Descriptive Statistics, with Comparative Data from 1969-70 and 1972-73 Surveys (Ann Arbor, MI: Institute for Social Research, 1979).

3. Paul O. Flaim and Howard N. Fullerton, Jr., "Labor Force Projections to 1990: Three Possible Paths," Monthly Labor Review (December 1978), pp. 25-33. "Americans Change: Demographics Affect the Economy," Business Week (February 20, 1978), pp. 64-77.

4. For these projections see, Ralph E. Smith, Women in the Labor Force in 1990 (Washington, DC: The Urban Institute, 1979).

5. This analysis is primarily based on data on earnings and occupational distribution of women working year round, full time, as compared to male workers. Despite the gains by some women in higher level positions, the wage differential in earnings between the sexes has persisted at basically the same rates from 1960-1977. Moreover, in general, women gain little in earnings over the life cycle as compared to men since their jobs lack similar advancement possibilities. See: Testimony of Alexis Herman, Nancy Barratt, "The Coming Decade: American Women and Human Resource Politics and Programs, 1979," Hearings before the Committee on Labor and Human Resources, 96th Congress, 1st session (January 31 and February 1, 1979), pp. 353, 1042. See also, Mary C. Dunlap, "The Legal Road to Equal Employment Opportunity: A Critical View," and Barbara B. Reagen, "De Facto Job Segregation," in Anne Foote Cahn, ed., Women in the U.S. Labor Force, Report for the Joint Economic Committee (New York, NY: Praeger, 1978).

6. Ruth Gilbert Shaeffer and Edith F. Lynton, Corporate Experiences in Improving Women's Job Opportunities, Conference Board Report #755 (New York, NY: The Conference Board, 1979).

7. Patricia Cayo Sexton, Women and Work, Employment and Training Administration R&D Monograph #46 (Washington, DC: Government Printing Office, 1977), pp. 1, 9-10.

8. These data refer to usage as of May 1980. Unless otherwise noted, information in this section is found in U.S. Bureau of Labor Statistics, News Release, February 24, 2981. The

definition used was phrased as "flextime or some other schedule that allows workers to vary the time they begin and end work."

9. Janice Neipert Hedges, "Flexible Schedules: Points and Issues," Monthly Labor Review, v. 100 (February 1977), p. 62.

10. New Schedules for a Changing Society, Work in America Institute (Scarsdale, NY: 1981), p. 34. On the issues arising from these differences, see Hedges, note 9, pp. 64-65.

11. See note #8.

12. Harriet Gorlin, Personnel Practices II: Hours of Work, Pay Practices, Relocation, Information Bulletin #92 (New York, NY: The Conference Board, 1981), Table 3.

13. Bureau of National Affairs, Bulletin to Management: ASPA-BNA Survey No. 25. Part-Time and Temporary Employees (Washington, DC: Bureau of National Affairs, 1974), reported in New Schedules for a Changing Society, p. 30.

14. John Owen, "Why Part Time Workers Tend to be in Low Jobs," Monthly Labor Review, Vol. 103 (June 1978), p. 12.

15. See note #7, pp. 29-30. According to Bureau of Labor Statistics data, the rate of absenteeism for single women in 1980 was approximately the same as that of men. Occupation and union membership also account for differential rates. (See: News, Department of Labor, Bureau of Labor Statistics, January 26, 1981.) In regard to tenure, Bureau of Labor Statistics reports during the period 1973-1978 no differences for men and women in the early years of labor force participation, with a widening differential increasing with age. Women had the highest tenure

rates in professional, technical and kindred fields and approximately the same job attachment as men in operative (nontransport) occupations. (See: News, Department of Labor, Bureau of Labor Statistics, April 23, 1979.)

16. For case studies of these experiences see: Stanley D. Nollen, New Work Schedules in Practice (New York, NY: Van Nostrand Reinhold/Work in America Institute Series, 1982) and Maureen E. McCarthy and Gail S. Rosenberg, Work Sharing: Case Studies (Kalamazoo, MI: The W. E. Upjohn Institute for Employment Research, 1981).

17. Gretl S. Meier, Job Sharing (Kalamazoo, MI: The W. E. Upjohn Institute, 1979).

18. See note #12, Table 5. The survey found that 6 percent of the 541 respondent firms have job sharing arrangements but there was no indication of the number of teams in each organization. A 1981 survey of 104 human resource executives of the Fortune 1300 by Louis Harris and Associates, Inc. found a high degree of interest in job sharing (and other flexible patterns). Of the policies considered likely to be adopted in the next five years, job sharing was indicated by most (70 percent) of the respondents. General Mills American Family Report 1980-81, FAMILIES AT WORK: Strengths and Strains (Minneapolis, MN: General Mills).

19. See: Gretl S. Meier, "Professionals and Supervisors as Part-Timers and Job Sharers" in Nollen, cited in footnote 16, pp. 59-68.

20. This summary is based largely on papers of the Worker Education and Training Policies Project of the National Institute of Work and Learning (formerly the National Manpower Institute), Washington, DC, 1980. See especially Harold

Goldstein, Training and Education by Industry. Also of interest are: Denise Wilder, Issues in Education and Training for Working Women, and Jane Shore, Alternative Work Patterns: Implications for Education and Training.

21. Irwin L. Goldstein, "Training in Work Organizations," Annual Reviews of Psychology (1980), 31: p. 234.

22. Goldstein, cited in footnote 20, p. 34.

23. Harriet Gorlin, Personnel Practices I: Recruitment, Placement, Training Communication, Information Bulletin #89 (New York, NY: The Conference Board, 1981), Table 34.

24. Ivan Charner, Kathleen Knox, Allen E. LeBel, Herbert Levine and Jane Shore, An Untapped Resource: Negotiated Tuition Aid in the Private Sector (Washington, DC: National Manpower Institute, 1978).

25. Mimi Abramovitz, Where Are the Women? Study of Worker Underutilization of Tuition-Refund Plans (Cornell University: New York State School of Industrial and Labor Relations, December 1977).

II. ADJUSTING WORK HOURS FOR EDUCATION
AND TRAINING: SOME RECENT EXPERIENCE

The following review of recent experience relating flexible work patterns to learning opportunities is based primarily on interviews and preliminary data collected in 1981 at selected worksites. It indicates certain additional information needed for more comprehensive investigation. More important, it implies the pre-conditions for policy consideration of this linkage.

Part Time: Progress and Problems

As already suggested, increasing participation in education and training through part-time schedules for low status women poses a contradiction. Obviously, some women who work part time are able to undertake continuing education, particularly with the growth of community colleges and other institutions offering low fees and convenient scheduling. But most women who voluntarily work part time do so in order to stretch nonwork hours to care for home and family. The majority, those at lower job levels, rarely have financial means of their own to return to school. Like many women working full time, they must also overcome fears of new learning situations. They, especially, will need the incentive of potential economic return.

To what degree have the efforts to improve the status, advancement opportunities, salary and fringe benefits of part-time employment succeeded so that reduced hours may serve as a bridge for learning? Certainly, the current picture causes less optimism than that of other new work patterns.

Opportunities for employer-sponsored training for part timers are unusual. If 80 percent of women working full time are confined to traditional female occupations, despite the changes outlined earlier, a still larger proportion of part-time workers remains even more stereotyped. Employers who are unlikely to invest in on-site training for such full-time workers are even less concerned with part timers. In fact, the expansion of part-time schedules is clearly limited by employers' concerns about training costs; workers are on the job only half-time and the numbers to be trained are doubled. Companies who employ part timers, even on a permanent basis, on the other hand, often find that costs are negligible, precisely because they hire workers who are either already trained or who need little or no training to perform their tasks.

Tuition Aid Benefits

Although an increasing number of employers are offering fringe benefits to part timers, these benefits usually take the form of paid holidays and vacations. A good deal of the reportedly "new" part-time employment, which affects women in predominantly female occupations, is often a convenience in "mother's hours," a genuine accommodation in time and place. These special arrangements rarely, however, include financial support for continued learning nor encouragement for upward mobility.

An example of this type of accommodation is found in the Control Data bindery plant, itself an innovative approach to job creation, in Selby, Minnesota. Established after the riots of the 60s, the plant was designed to provide employment in the inner-city area. In mid-1981, the 280 employees, largely minority and female, all worked part time although their managers worked full time. (In the organization as a whole, about 60 percent of the 56,000 employees have some control over their work hours. About 5,000 are part timers, including many in professional positions.) At the bindery, skill requirements are low, and mothers, teenagers and other students work three shifts as needed. Although in the past ten years about 175 employees have moved to higher-paying, full-time jobs in the company and elsewhere, management regards this plant operation only incidentally as a training mechanism. Moreover, even if continued education or formal training were wished for by employers, company policy does not include these part timers as "supplementals" in eligibility for financial assistance.

In general, even where employers provide tuition aid programs, part timers are usually ineligible for these benefits. The Conference Board survey cited earlier, which found that a large majority of the companies surveyed offered tuition aid to full-time workers, also found that part-time production workers were eligible in programs offered by only 6 percent of the firms (compared with eligibility to their full-time counterparts by 93 percent of these firms). Programs which included part-time clerical workers were offered by 13 percent or survey respondents (compared to 99 percent for their full-time counterparts); most were in banking and insurance. 1/

The companies investigated in this study which employ a substantial proportion of part-time workers present a varied picture. Some limit benefits to full timers only; others provide for part-time entitlement, and still others, even where career development programs exist, limit the types of courses open to less-than-full-time workers.

Part Time and Tuition Aid: An Experiment
in Data Collection

In an effort to test the feasibility of determining participation by part timers, we examined the tuition assistance records at Santa Clara County, California, of 367 employees represented by Local 715 of the Service Employees International Union (SEIU). This site and employee population are particularly relevant because the union local, which represents about 58 percent of the county's workforce, includes a high proportion of workers in low paying jobs. The local, an oft-cited example of positive union leadership in worktime flexibility, had negotiated for a minimum number of part-time positions ("split" codes), whereby two employees divide the responsibility of a full-time position and still receive full fringe benefits. It also successfully bargained for a program of Voluntary Reduced Work Hours (VRWH) whereby employees may choose at six-month intervals, reductions in worktime. These range from 2.5 percent to 20 percent, with corresponding wage reductions but with seniority and fringe benefits largely unchanged.

According to tuition aid records, those employees who work either split codes or reduced hours (in almost equal numbers) do, in fact, participate in outside education in a much higher proportion (18 percent) than might be expected by their representation in the Local 715 population (6-7 percent).

This is especially noteworthy because of other factors influencing the use of tuition aid funds: (1) Employees do not usually need to use such schedules to enroll in the few courses made possible under the relatively low reimbursement sum ($300 at that time). The county permits workers, in those instances when a class is not offered on non-worktime, to make up only half of the time taken from work. (2) All employees are using the funds less than in previous years when programs were better publicized and fewer free programs were offered by local colleges. (3) Training is given a low priority at all levels of the organization. These activities might now be considered more important because budget cuts have resulted in limited staff and changed assignments. Management regards the allocation of training funds, however, as a luxury in contrast to direct service needs.

Data Needs

A preliminary study of these records also made clear, however, the many categories of additional data required for valid analysis of the effect of reduced schedules on participation in outside education. More comprehensive information would disclose, for example: (1) the extent to which participation may be affected by the ineligibility of employees in certain departments and job classifications to work less than full time; (2) how the 20 percent usage rate by female participants on reduced schedules in lower level jobs (clerks, hospital, social and community service workers) compares with their representation in the population; and (3) whether the largest (35 percent) group of the participants, public health nurses, were also using the additional time off for which they are eligible through a separate plan.

Job-Sharing: Existing Limitations

Investigation of the effect of other examples of job sharing as a means to increase participation in educational opportunities poses particular complications in regard to women in low status jobs. Knowledge is limited because the practices, despite efforts of its advocates, continue as an accommodation to individual employees, with only small numbers in a growing diversity of worksites. Among these experiences are many in which individuals have deliberately chosen to use the option to pursue further learning. 2/ In others, job-sharing arrangements have allowed the pairing of employees with different skill levels, with one partner training the other.

But, in the rare instances involving larger numbers of employees (50 plus), job sharing has either been directed only at high school students in a cooperative program (Equitable Life Insurance), or utilized the pattern as a temporary alternative to lay-offs (United Airlines).

In general, both the more singular and larger scale examples have demonstrated the difficulty of utilizing job sharing as it is now most commonly practiced as a means to significantly increase access to education and training opportunities. Perception and practice too often resemble the more traditional part-time arrangements. With few exceptions, companies initiate job sharing experiments by allowing the option only to current full-time employees. Where new hires are permitted, employees are usually already trained. And, although some higher level jobs are being opened to sharing, employers still tend to restructure jobs perceived as easily divisible, those likely to be at the lower salary levels and lacking advancement possibilities.

These limitations are exemplified at the Rolscreen Company in Pella, Iowa, an unusual instance of job sharing by production workers. About 4 percent of the workforce (68 individuals), predominantly women, arrange half-time schedules with partners. They choose to job share primarily to make time for family care or more leisure or to ease the transition to retirement. Although a few sharers are students working a night shift, normally part timers are not eligible for the 100 percent tuition reimbursement which is used by about 10 percent of all workers at the plant. Company policy limits job sharing to those previously employed full time and these only in job classifications below the higher skill levels.

In order for job sharing to become a valid means to continue learning, future practice must first verify that the option can, in fact, fulfill its promise to open positions in a wider variety of occupations and levels than has so far been the case. At this time, job sharing at higher level jobs has not caught hold in industry or business nor existed for a sufficient period in the public sector to determine whether even this form of part-time employment can provide genuine career progression.

Although some sharers have been promoted, these are likely to be cases in which one partner moves to a full-time position; rarely are both promoted as sharers. In such instances, still small scale, the shared job has itself served as training. But, given the complex nature of divided responsibility in higher level positions, it is still unknown whether and by what means such positions will remain open to sharing beyond the tenure of initial incumbents.

If, in the future, part-time employment, including job sharing, permits vertical and occupational mobility, then these reduced hours might more realistically provide both impetus and means for continued learning. A longer tenure and a lower turnover through a more continuous shift to and from full-time employment within the same firm could also then be possible. Because this kind of life-long employment would focus investment on the employee rather than on the job per se, it would increase the incentive in education and training for both the employer and the employee.

40-Hour Flexible Schedules

Compressed Work Schedules

A few examples of the shortened workweek indicate a more immediately practical link to education and training and suggest the particular conditions which need apply. In all of these organizations, management is committed to policies of employee development and use of tuition aid is high. In only two, however, have employees found this particular work pattern especially effective.

At the Connecticut General Insurance Company, a forerunner in developing employee programs aimed at increasing satisfaction, a variety of training and education programs are open to nonexempt workers. Generally, although no formal flextime programs exist, employees are allowed time off (or compensatory time) for on-site or off-site programs. Production workers, however, such as those employed at the Data Center, find this especially difficult. About 170 employees (15 percent of Center employees) work a shift of three 12-hour days. Although no data are available on their participation, the managers of training programs and the data unit indicate that employees do take advantage of training on their free days. Future investigation would have to take into account not only the comparative use of tuition aid, but also the participation in internal courses paid from the separate department budgets.

A different experience has taken place at the Wells Fargo Bank (San Francisco), an organization also noted for its career development programs for women. Here, worktime flexibility is encouraged in arrangements by individual departments, although again no official flextime policy exists. Several years ago, the Trust Department attempted to institute a four-day week. The Department, according to its manager, is more inclined than others to experiment, possibly as a reaction to its pure service nature and its relatively rigid work content. It also has a high education budget, of which tuition assistance is only one part.

The four-day schedule proved unsuccessful because of problems of coordination within the bank and the need to meet particular state requirements for certain employee hours. But the department also found that employees did not wish to schedule courses on "free" time, particularly when an estimated 10 to 15 percent of time at work is ordinarily concerned with education and training. Employees in lower level jobs, particularly, may feel less incentive to volunteer for education, it was explained, because their isolation from the rest of the organization and their highly specialized skills make mobility to other departments unusual.

A more successful use of compressed schedules takes place at Physio-Control, a medical instrumentation company in Redmond, Washington. The company had earlier operated four-day and four-and-a-half-day shifts; it added a weekend shift of three 12-hour days because of labor shortages and a high use of overtime. Because the work is technically oriented and highly skilled, Physio-Control was particularly anxious to attract students and others interested in continued training. At the same time, it encouraged the local community college to develop relevant courses, especially in electronics and in accounting.

The percentage of weekend workers ("weekend warriors") using the 100 percent work-related tuition reimbursement has varied from 35 percent to 65 percent, considerably higher than the approximate 15 percent participation by all employees. However, numbers are small and only a few of the 42 workers on this shift (which accounts for 15 percent of the total employee population) are women.

Flextime
        Although we know too little yet about which workers on flextime schedules also use the option in order to pursue education and training, this new work pattern appears to offer the most significant potential for increasing participation by nonexempt as well as exempt workers. Two surveys of government workers have found that employees on flextime schedules realized the greatest advantages in increasing personal time for family and recreation, as would be expected. But, additionally, a large portion of the survey groups (43 percent, 49 percent) also found that the schedules afforded a greater amount of time for educational activities. 3/

        The results of a similar survey at the John Hancock Insurance Company in Boston are of special interest because they reveal that, although 19 percent of the workers on flextime felt the new pattern increased time for educational pursuits, 72 percent of the survey group found that flextime had little impact. 4/ No valid comparison can be made with government surveys without additional data, but it might be pointed out that at John Hancock, overall use of tuition assistance was only about 1 percent (1980-81). Moreover, in contrast to the experience described below where flextime may extend training time, at John Hancock it serves instead to limit the time available for in-house programs. In order not to penalize employees on such time schedules, supervisors confine training courses to core hours.

Hewlett-Packard: Possibilities and Data Needs

A different approach may emerge at Hewlett-Packard (HP), the California electronics firm, where anticipated growth and explicit corporate philosophy are contributing to consideration of revised employee development policies. Technically, all employees may use flextime schedules, although use is universal in manufacturing and unusual in sales. Several personnel and training managers at headquarters and in at least one division where interviews were conducted acknowledge that flexible hours may significantly increase participation in education and training opportunities.

Flextime has "opened more options, though not necessarily more time," explained a training manager. It may allow an employee to start work two hours earlier or to stop work later and take advantage of either education sponsored off-site or company training on-site. The schedule also enables the company to put classes on "the front or tail end of shifts and pick up employees on the graveyard shift at the same time."

We would need much more data, however, at each divisional level to determine whether and in what ways this more flexible learning time affects the large number of women employed at Hewlett-Packard. Of the 47,000 HP employees in the U.S., almost half are women (41.5 U.S., 43.5 Bay Area). They are concentrated in the nonexempt population at the secretarial and semiskilled jobs. Their mobility beyond the nonexempt level in this typically male-dominated, high-tech organization has generally been limited to management positions in personnel and occasionally in marketing. Whether they (and the men in lower skilled categories) would take advantage of more flexibly scheduled education and training depends on the extent to which the company may develop and encourage these opportunities at each of its 43 divisions--where such innovation generally takes place.

Training activities, now directed at management, may focus in the near future on the development of production workers. "One of our biggest issues," the director of personnel maintained, "is the need for trained people, technicians as well as engineers." Employees will have to be moved up into the hard-to-fill higher skilled jobs. "There's no reason," he pointed out, "that we can't get entry level production people moving up if they're interested and we make it easy."

Continued growth is stimulating changes in the content of employee development programs; the existing courses aimed primarily at familiarizing employees with the organization may be supplemented by others in more specific job content. The results of "Open Line," a 1979 employee attitude survey, were widely reported in the house magazine. They are frequently referred to by personnel managers in discussions of education and training needs. This survey, which disclosed employee desire for skill training and counseling, has also served to raise the expectations of nonexempt employees, in the opinion of at least one manager.

Other changes affect the scheduling of training. Until recently, all skill training has had to take place on workers' own time. A greater number of courses are now being offered on company time as well as in off-hours programs. Off-hours programs are taught by company instructors on-site and are generally considered to strictly benefit the employee, although they may also include general skill training. Beyond the San Francisco Bay area, at least three divisions are operating joint programs with community colleges whereby college credit courses are taught by college teachers on company sites.

Data Needs

In order to investigate participation in the on-site, after-hours training programs and to determine whether flextime in fact increases opportunities, future investigation should obtain data from a sampling of selected divisions. To consider which types of opportunities are actually available, these data should also include information on the varying employee populations at each location in comparison with the extent to which the types of courses differ by entity and locality.

For example, according to the data for the North Bay Area in California (seven divisions), the participation rate in after-hours courses is low (3 percent of those eligible), compared with other areas where it may be as high as 35 percent. Two possible explanations were offered: (1) that the North Bay Area includes a higher percentage of clerical workers (who are presumably less inclined to pursue technical courses which are offered); and (2) in this same geographic area, a higher percentage of employees may be participating in courses at community colleges rather than in those conducted on-site. At least one area college has scheduled special "Early Bird" morning courses which may accommodate employees either on flextime or on regular schedules.

In order to determine how the amount spent for tuition aid ($2 million in fiscal 1980) was actually dispersed, it would be necessary to examine data beyond those available at headquarters. An accounting of the dollar amounts expended by each entity does not accurately reflect employee participation, since: (1) costs for outside education vary by site, and (2) budgets at each site are used in varying amounts by individual employees. More detailed information at selected sites would also provide a basis to analyze the comparative use of a prorated time reimbursement scheme by which HP refunds 100 percent of the expense (assumed to be the usual use) if personal time is used for classroom work, 50 percent if company time is used, and 75 percent if time is shared between the employee and the company.

Informal Flexibility

A comprehensive study of the role of new work patterns should also examine the more informal flexibility in those workplaces where a large proportion of lower status employees takes part in continuing learning. In these companies, schedules are adjusted either in an ad hoc fashion or on a regular basis through released time. 5/ Although such practice defies precise quantification, intensive on-site investigation would better determine the equity of access within employee populations and the result on employee and employer of this intent-specific time flexibility. Policymakers might then more rationally assess the relative advantages of new worktime patterns. It is important to recognize, however, that this informal flexibility is most likely to be made available to employees in low status jobs when companies have broad, well-developed programs in education and training already in place.

Polaroid: Opportunities and Participation

At the Polaroid Corporation in Cambridge, Massachusetts, women working at hourly jobs take part in large numbers in innovative internal and external education and training programs. 6/ Participation on company and employee time is high in this atmosphere where "education is in the air."

The success of the overall program has depended on several factors: (1) the company's financial success and corresponding growth from 200 employees in 1957 to 13,000 (1981), with many employees in jobs requiring both technical skills and good general education; (2) the initial commitment to education and training of its founder, Edwin Land, in his desire to create a model business enterprise; (3) policies of internal promotion and job posting; (4) a community in which many educational facilities are available; and (5) careful staff planning and execution of programs.

At the time of this study, about half of all Polaroid employees were involved in one or more of the internal and external education programs provided and paid for by the company. In external courses alone, about 10 percent of employees participated, well over the national average in tuition assistance programs. This has been attributed to program structure, content and support. Full costs are paid in advance (rather than the more usual reimbursement procedure) and hourly and salaried employees are entitled to the same benefits. The program is well publicized and includes staff support to assist and advise employees. Content is broadly based so as to include not only skill improvement but also basic courses in reading and math as well as others leading to associate, bachelor, and advanced degrees.

Tuition aid finances company-initiated training programs requiring education outside as well as courses undertaken by employees in external programs. Several special career mobility programs combine both in-house and external courses. Some involve women workers: the nine-month secretarial internship program, and, to a lesser degree, the more unusual two-year internal technical cooperative program whereby a small number of employees receive two-thirds pay and alternate periods of work and study toward a bachelor of science degree.

Data Needs

Data available during this writing suggest that further investigation might yield useful information to examine the relationship of time schedules to education and training for women in low status jobs. According to Polaroid managers, use of tuition aid by nonexempt workers in mid-1981 was approximately 40 percent. But we would need to know more precisely the number of women participating, the jobs they occupy, the types of courses they pursue, and the results on mobility and well-being.

In internal programs, women have been well represented: approximately 20 percent of the total population of nonexempt women engaged in internal courses at this time were women in hourly jobs (compared to their representation in the company population of about 25 percent). According to training managers, most hourly workers take courses in technical math and manufacturing skills, English as a second language and in secretarial techniques. More specific data would be required to determine the types and number of courses which each employee undertakes as well as the number of employees who apply and/or who do not complete courses.

More important, policymakers must have more
complete data on the effects of participation in
these programs. A report by the National
Commission on Working Women has questioned
whether, in fact, the availability of
opportunities has had as significant results on
the mobility of women in lower-level jobs at
Polaroid as in other organizations. 7/

Tektronix: A Singular Success Story?
    The innovative education and training programs
open to all employees at Tektronix (Tek), an
electronics company in Beaverton, Oregon, have had
significant effect on moving lower status
employees to new jobs and job levels. 8/ "My
goal," explained the manager in charge of these
programs, "is to help people get involved in
education that will help them to help themselves,
to understand more about [the company's] products,
their jobs and the jobs they would like to have."
Many of the men who have become vice presidents
started at benchwork. Women, who account for
almost half of all employees, have often been
first employed as production, assembly line,
secretarial and clerical workers. From 1975 to
1980, when the number of employees more than
doubled, the number of women who moved to
professional jobs more than tripled. In 1980,
almost 30 percent of managers were women, compared
with 8 percent in 1975.

    Flexibility is an integral part of the Tek
atmosphere. Although many courses take place
after work (except for immediate skill training),
employees may also occasionally use worktime for
learning. In this informal, largely democratic
workplace, an honor system allows employees to
keep their own time records. Employees may change
to part-time schedules, though their numbers
appear low; fewer than 10 percent use flextime,
which, as a manager commented, "happens anyway."

These informal adjustments, however, are only one of the several factors which have made Tek education and training programs so effective. Other factors include: (1) a policy of internal promotion which encourages the linking of learning to career paths; (2) an active staff in the education and training department to counsel and assist employees; (3) low cost of internal on-site courses; and (4) the provision of child care.

Because of its location in a relatively remote area, initial labor shortages virtually assured that the company had to "develop its own." Tek founders Howard Vollum and Jack Murdock, who organized the company in 1946 as a profit sharing venture, believed that the long term success of the company depended in large measure on encouraging employees to develop their career potential. This philosophy has continued to underlie company policy, even though the more recent presence of other electronics companies and of community colleges has somewhat lessened earlier needs.

An increasing number of women participate in the Tek Education Program (TEP), in noncredit courses aimed at providing the skills for higher job levels. Although most classes take place on-site after-hours, a few are held during the workday to allow second shift employees to take part. The company pays half of the low ($20) fee. Child care is available and employee family members may also participate.

The tuition aid program, which allows both work and nonwork-related education, has been well used. Overall participation in 1980 was about 13 percent, somewhat higher in the field offices than in the main facility in Beaverton where TEP and other on-site classes are held. Women employees use about half of the aid, it is estimated.

Courses are scheduled in regular classes at community colleges but with registration at Tek or in the cooperative education programs sponsored jointly with local institutions. Most employees (70 percent) use the full 100 percent reimbursement for job-related courses rather than the 50 percent offered for nonwork-related courses.

These internal and external programs (together with special workshops for upward and occupational change) are made effective because of the company's linkage of education and training to career paths. The catalogue which summarizes courses and reimbursement procedures for tuition assistance also outlines possible job and career opportunities. It explains how courses may be used to attain a new job, cautioning that "although no class or education course guarantees a job, most are helpful." The handbook describes positions, indicates what types of opportunities are available to enter this field, lists potential earnings or pay raises and specifies courses in the TEP program while also suggesting that many courses are available at local community colleges.

A system of job posting and career counseling also supports education and training programs. Despite some recent tightening of regulations, the Job Opportunity transfer system, which is widely distributed through the company newsletter, has facilitated lateral as well as upward moves by all employees, including women in lower level jobs. The career change process has been fluid. Tek encourages informal discussions with managers, especially because managers have often changed careers during their employment at Tek and are likely to be receptive to employee needs. The company has also periodically added more formal career counseling and special career related workshops and programs to meet specific needs.

The experiences at Tektronix and at Polaroid extend the possible scope of future consideration of workplace flexibility and learning—particularly for lower status workers. These adjustments in worktime may be, <u>under such circumstances</u>, as valuable as are the particular <u>flexible</u> patterns. The additional data noted would provide a better basis for examining the equity of opportunity and indicate its effects. But, however broadly it defines flexibility, subsequent study will also need to assess the implications of some of the fundamental organizational issues which have emerged during this review of current experience.

NOTES

1. See note #I-23, Table 35. Although the survey included data on participation, no breakdown was made between full and part time workers.

2. Gretl S. Meier, "The Effects of New Work Patterns on Family Life and on Men and Women as Individuals," in Stanley Nollen, <u>New Work Schedules in Practice</u>, Work in America Institute (New York, NY: Van Nostrand Reinhold, 1982).

3. <u>Flextime: Evaluation of a One-Year Experiment at the U.S. Geological Survey</u>. Prepared by the Branch Management Analysis, Administrative Division, U.S. Geological Survey (Reston, VA: August 1977); <u>Evaluation of Alternative Work Schedules</u>, National Oceanic and Atmospheric Administration (Washington, DC: January 1981).

4. <u>Four-Day Workweek and Flextime Survey Report</u>, John Hancock Mutual Life Insurance Company, Personnel Research Operations (Boston, MA: August 12, 1978) mimeo.

5. In two of the surveys on tuition aid usage, "adjusted time" is listed as a separate category from paid or nonpaid time. A 1979 survey of 141 plans found that about 8 percent of those companies which allow workers to take time off for courses pay employees for time lost; 10 percent grant employees time off without pay; 14 percent adjust work schedules and 8 percent use flexible schedules. Allen E. LeBel, A Study of Negotiated Tuition Aid in Industry, Exhibit V (Washington, DC: National Manpower Institute, January 1978) unpublished. A more consistent survey (adjusted for nonresponse) found that, of the 274 companies with tuition aid programs, 12 percent of the respondent companies "adjusted schedules" for office and clerical workers, 11 percent for production workers. (See note #I-23.)

6. For a detailed description see Kathleen Knox, Polaroid Corporation's Tuition Assistance Plan: A Case Study, Worker Education and Training Policies Project, National Institute of Work and Learning (Washington, DC, 1979).

7. See Appendix, Mobility in the Marketplace. Case studies of Programs, Policies and Practices that Provide Working Women with Career Mobility, Draft Manuscript (Washington, DC: National Commission on Working Women, 1981).

8. Useful background material on Tektronix is found in Paul Ferrini and L. Allen Parker, Career Change (Cambridge, MA: Technical Education Research Centers, 1978), and Mobility in the Marketplace, note 7.

III. FUTURE RESEARCH:
SOME CONSIDERATIONS

This preliminary study has found positive, albeit tentative, connections between flexible hours and employer-sponsored learning programs. It has also suggested, however, that this linkage will affect <u>women in low status jobs</u> on a significant scale only if other conditions also prevail.

In the immediate future, patterns within the 40-hour workweek--the compressed week and flextime--appear the more practicable. Even the potential advantages of flextime, the most promising work schedule, however, are likely to be best realized when companywide, <u>well-developed</u> education and training programs are already in place. Part-time arrangements, in contrast, must first accord these employees eligibility to programs comparable to their full-time counterparts. Considering the current economic scene, the requisite expansion of part-time jobs which would encourage more continuous employment, i.e., a more regularized transition to and from full-time employment, now remains far more doubtful.

To be of value to policymakers, any subsequent research should be broader in scope than was originally conceived by this paper. It must take into account: (1) the worktime-learning connection for employees at all job levels, men as well as women; (2) the practice of informal flexibility as well as the use of the particular schedules; (3) the shorter and longer range effects on well-being and mobility as perceived by <u>employees</u> as well as employers; and (4) the contributory role of other organizational strategies to encourage mobility, including ongoing support systems.

A more comprehensive investigation might also be narrower in focus. Education and training of nonmanagement personnel, a comparatively recent concern, is translated into consistent practice by relatively few organizations. The degree to which such enterprises may also utilize time flexibility to enhance participation depends in large part on the stage of its commitment to employee development. In order to determine the value of flexibility as one variable, subsequent study would best confine itself to a selected few organizations which have reached a more advanced stage. Management at these worksites has a more impelling rationale to examine education and training programs and to make available the necessary data.

Contained, in-depth studies at selected preliminary sites would determine more conclusively the feasibility of such schedules to enhance opportunities for low status as well as other workers. The County of Santa Clara, for example, offers various time schedules, a diverse employee population and an active union leadership. Its experience might provide a replicable example for private as well as public organizations, particularly as training funds are affected by cost reductions. Further investigation elsewhere, such as at Hewlett-Packard and Tektronix, would yield data for a more valid analysis of the capability of different approaches to promote employee development in the high-technology growth industry.

But beyond additional data and specific site selection, consideration of the feasibility of new patterns to increase learning and of future research toward this end might also take into account some broader implications of this preparatory study: the effects of organizational complexity, industry-education cooperation, differences between during- and after-hours scheduling, and changing organizational policies.

Organizational Complexity

It is especially important that subsequent study consider policy and process within the entire organization, rather than at corporate headquarters alone. Companies offering education and training tend to be large, with complex structure at headquarters and several separate worksites. Continuing decentralization will further diversify personnel practices as rising costs to employers and employees discourage geographic mobility. Education and training and flexible worktime opportunities now vary widely within the same company, a result of (1) the size and function of each entity and its units, (2) occupational and job categories and levels, (3) the proximity of outside education facilities and, not least, (4) the inclinations of individual managers and supervisors.

The initiation of innovative training opportunities and of worktime flexibility may more likely occur at local levels. An in-depth study of Hewlett-Packard, for example, would examine how pervasive is the type of program in progress at one of its 43 divisions and what might be necessary conditions. The Computer Systems Division in Cupertino was (at the time of this study) directed by a personnel manager especially concerned with increasing opportunities for nonexempt workers. He had developed, in addition to the more usual apprenticeships, a special program to train these employees to move to entry level engineering positions. Half of the participating employees were women, former secretaries and production workers who worked half time at regular pay and returned to school full time for a two-year period.

Elsewhere, in female-intensive industries (even in companies with active career development programs), eligibility for in-house and external education and training may vary substantially among employee groups. At John Hancock, agency field employees (about half of the total 20,000 U.S. employees) are unable to participate in courses reimbursed by tuition aid. Regulations confine eligibility only to those employees on the home office payroll. (The company has been considering extending eligibility to at least the clerical workers in field offices, particularly because they also lack opportunities in the career development program available to their counterparts employed at headquarters.)

In banking especially, the types of training opportunities are affected by geographic spread as well as by the traditional separation of functions at the branch levels. The Bank of America, the largest U.S. bank (highly rated for its employment of women as managers and officials), relies on job posting rather than on formal upgrading programs for office and clerical workers. Nor is it possible for corporate staff to oversee the way its training programs are used at branch levels. At Wells Fargo (noted earlier as a reportedly exemplary model of mobility for women) the in-house career development program, or "catalogue" courses, have been used primarily by employees at headquarters. Occasionally, branch employees on the "platform" or credit side, rather than those who are "operational" (tellers) may take part. The staff development guide, designed to encourage training of these other branch employees by managers, emphasizes that "interest in employees' career goals will pay significant dividends in staff morale and performance." However, here, as in all highly decentralized organizations, branch managers have substantial flexibility in the amount of training they develop.

This same complexity also complicates company efforts to systematize data on training, tuition assistance and on the use of flexible hours. At Wells Fargo, for example, some managers maintain that the thousand accounting units with separate budgets would require a "Cadillac system of accounting" to track how much is spent and for which employee in outside seminars, internal programs and tuition assistance. Elsewhere, organizations have only started to establish computerized personnel records. Some, like John Hancock, are prompted by the need for performance appraisals. In others, where employee development plans are less defined, managers are only now establishing methods to organize training data in order to stimulate supervisor interest in new training programs.

Industry-Education Cooperation

Subsequent investigation might also take account of the effects of the changing relationship between employers and educational institutions. Although in-house learning programs remain their highest investment, many companies are also turning to educational institutions to fulfill some of their training needs. Community colleges, especially, are seeking older students, including a large part of the working population, as the golden years of the 1970s turn to the declining enrollment of the 1980s. This new relationship is requiring added efforts by each sector to increase flexibility.

It is important to realize, of course, that only some of these programs involve nonexempt workers. The largest part of employee-sponsored degree programs and short courses affect managers and professionals and are therefore not relevant

to this study. Peripheral, but of interest for
future research as they may be applicable to a
greater range of employees, are the flexible but
limited term work-study schemes for high school
students. In these, firms may fulfill a sense of
community responsibility and also attract
graduates to hard-to-find jobs.

The availability of low cost courses at local
educational institutions may affect the
development of internal training programs for
nonexempt workers in several respects. It may
serve to explain a certain lack of management
interest in such programs, as appears the case at
Hewlett-Packard. At Polaroid, however, the
presence of such institutions gives added impetus
to the internal courses which serve to prepare
employees for outside programs. At Tektronix, the
more recent establishment of local colleges has
changed the content of internal education.
General education and cultural classes, which were
introduced when internal programs were first
initiated, were later eliminated as community
college courses became more available. The
internal program, which then became more
occupationally oriented, may in the future be
expanded if, as anticipated, local outside sources
are forced by budget cuts to reduce offerings.

Industry-education cooperation also bears on
flexibility in both place and time. Probably only
a relatively few companies assist employees with
registration for courses taken off-site, but many
more appear to be using the worksite for the
jointly sponsored after-hours courses. Although
instructors are usually company employees, credit
is often offered when courses are taught by
college faculty whose salary is also paid by the
college. This convenience, especially when
courses are offered immediately after worktime,
may be as helpful to workers as are the flexibly

scheduled classes taking place outside the workplace. In areas where no such scheduling exists, flextime will make little difference. But elsewhere (as the "Early Bird" classes mentioned before), class times are more likely to coincide with the varying schedules. Employees may start work earlier or later or organizations may include these hours as worktime to be used for on-site training.

Employers sponsor both general and job-specific courses at community colleges. The number of companies that reimburse employees for nonjob-related courses is probably low and it appears that employees are less prone to choose general education classes even when costs are covered (generally at the rate of 50 percent). Usually, companies reimburse the fees of specific job-related courses such as those which familiarize nonexempt workers with technical fields, i.e., as data processing, computer programming. But, they are also increasingly concerned with sharpening basic skills and technical writing, speed reading and math. "English as a Second Language" (ESL) courses tend to be offered in areas where employee populations include a number of recent immigrants.

Among the many issues which will be explored as organizations and educational institutions seek to insure that this cooperation brings mutual advantage is whether or not the traditional responsibility of these colleges can be maintained. On the one hand, industry-sponsored courses are needed to sustain enrollment. On the other, contracting with employers may also restrict the access of other adults including those who are not employees of the sponsoring firms. The potential danger also exists that the emphasis on vocational curriculum will further reduce the institutional resources which have been

devoted to broader general education. Because
many low status workers have had few past
opportunities for such learning, the result would
be to narrow even further their range of choice.

Worktime and NonWorktime Scheduling
     The feasibility of new work patterns to
increase participation in learning activities will
also be affected by policy variations on the use
of worktime or nonworktime. Flextime may increase
opportunities in both time arrangements, but its
value to employees will also depend on whether
employee or company time is involved.

     In regard to nonexempt workers, there are
indications that the content of training may be
changing, causing a wider range of activities to
take place on worktime. This is not to say, even
as at the management levels, that training extends
beyond immediate task orientation toward long term
intellectual and human development. Rather, its
vocational orientation may also encompass
long-range career development. Elsewhere and more
generally, employer-sponsored learning may include
the remedial basic education courses mentioned
earlier.

     As we have seen, companies vary widely in the
degree of responsibility they assume for this
enlarged content. At Hewlett-Packard, where even
skill training on company time is of recent
origin, reimbursement for outside learning is
limited to more narrow job-related subjects. In
contrast, at McGraw-Hill where a more broadly
educated workforce is deemed desirable, the
company maintains an active program of continuing
education--some 67 courses, many carrying college
credit. Here, too, these courses are scheduled
after work, in contrast to the worktime classes
which are described in the catalogue as "designed
for immediate application on the job or

preparation for a job the employees' department head hopes the employee can assume."

Courses on company time of a broader nature are apparently more available to nonexempt workers at those sites in female-intensive industries where career development programs have been instituted. At Wells Fargo, at least one-third of the internal courses are open to "staff." At Connecticut General, worktime courses affecting nonexempt employees include those in "individual development" (career management, etc.), others in "communication" (writing skills and ESL), as well as in "continuing education" (typing, math, and degree programs).

The scheduling of courses listed in Polaroid's "Human Resource Program for 1981" shows more diverse distinctions. Management courses all take place on company time as do the technical skill classes for nonexempt workers. The classes in word processing and secretarial skills vary so that seven take place on worktime, three on employee time, and two on shared hours. Of the ESL classes, ony one uses worktime, with two on employee time and three on shared time. Moreover, all those in "fundamental skills" (reading, writing, math, academic equivalency programs and tutor training) are on shared time. Company time is taken only in part, reportedly because supervisors do not regard these skills as immediately relevant. Even though managers may recognize that the lack presents problems, the acquisition of skills is not considered a company responsibility.

Future investigation might well examine the effect on participation of these varying schedules, particularly the use of shared time. The combined hours may be especially effective in increasing participation for upward mobility programs. At the State of Connecticut, which has developed programs involving clerical workers, this scheduling is considered appropriate because the employer "gives some incentive and yet employees have to make some sacrifice."

Further study, then, might explore the degree to which employees agree with some management perceptions of the limited potential of shared training time. The "infringement" of employees' time at a program at the United California Bank made for certain difficulties. A pilot program for secretaries at Wells Fargo was unsuccessful, reportedly because the women needed early evening hours for family responsibilities. At John Hancock, it was explained that training on worktime is difficult for production (i.e., clerical workers) and experiments with both shared and after-hours schedules proved unsuccessful. The problem was caused by the need for carpools for the longer commute beyond the immediate Boston area, and possibly also by the need for second jobs. At least one company also felt that the employees in operating areas, who have set work quotas, often consider training as an "escape from the workplace."

Changing Organizational Policies

Workers' experiences are affected by their place in the organizational system and also by where the system happens to be at that moment. Subsequent study of flexible work and learning might also be aware that, although only some firms are at an advanced stage of employee development, others appear to be in the process of change.

Of the organizations offering significant learning opportunities and/or alternative work patterns to lower status workers, few deliberately use flexibility formally in order to increase learning. But one of the unexpected findings of this preliminary study is that more firms than might be anticipated are recognizing the need for more broadly-based employee development. Some are considering new means to achieve this objective. If this process were to continue in even a few firms, changes which appear minor in the context of the total labor market may still be significant at the specific enterprise level.

Some few companies have progressed beyond the learning opportunities as we have defined them to alter work itself so that it becomes a learning experience. Although their examples may be distinctive, they provide a frame of reference for subsequent study. In these organizations, the introduction of socio-technic systems and job rotation has redesigned work so as to increase worker participation, learning opportunities and worktime flexibility.

The most highly publicized of these experiments has taken place at the Harmon Automotive Division Plant in Bolivar, Tennessee. Learning is both part of the job and more formal in classes at the Harmon School. Job redesign has increased participation in decisionmaking and in self-management for many workers who have had only a few years of formal schooling. As employees share in productivity increases, they have been able to earn free time. Many of these free hours have been used by employees to take part in classes. Since 1974 when the program started, enrollments have been high in courses of basic education, work-related or special interest courses and health and safety. 1/

This type of continuous learning, however, remains unusual in the U.S., where training is aimed for the next job rather than at the whole person (as is more likely in Japan). Only a small number of large companies have developed sophisticated training. Many more, especially those in the high technology growth industries, are in what may become the beginning stages of developing training programs.

In most companies, it is contended, management development is but the first step in the process. As managers at all levels become more skilled in "human relations," they tend to become aware of training needs and to gain the skills to put new training ideas into practice. At the Weyerhaeuser Company in Tacoma, Washington, for example, this has also taken the form of a new kind of training for first line supervisors. A program involving 350 employees which includes many nonexempt workers (those supervising a few others) is expected to spread to several thousand employees at headquarters and other locations.

Much of the attention to employee development needs, as we have discussed, has resulted from the existence of equal opportunity laws and regulations. Although the current political climate may substantially reduce implementation of earlier affirmative action guidelines, certain change processes have been started. In the recent past, only a part of this change has involved education and training directly. Many companies have improved formal training whereby some in-house training is available to all interested employees and extended eligibility under tuition assistance to include work-related rather than only job-related courses.

Of more importance, equal opportunity issues have often had to be dealt with in the larger context of overall personnel policies and practices. 2/ These concerns have also been addressed as a matter for the whole organization rather than the personnel department alone, particularly because the response to affirmative

action has come through regular job openings
rather than through special programming. All
levels of management have had to be involved to
some extent in planning and implementation. As
an additional result, certain interpersonal
barriers have been lowered in some instances.
Women have gained not only the opportunity to
learn new technical skills, but also greater
familiarity with what one manager has described as
"corporate street sense."

The introduction by firms of new means of
"communication," especially quality circles, may
also have long-range effects on expanding
management awareness of the concerns of low status
employees. When employees meet together to solve
the problems of the workplace, they are encouraged
to open broader dialogue. Experiments with
quality circles, as a senior vice president of the
Bank of America commented, may also provide an
added type of development skill for low status
employees, a more effective exposure. Managers,
especially at the corporate level, "may begin to
look at employees differently and change their
sense of lower expectation."

All the requisite conditions which will, in
the future, determine the applicability of new
work patterns to broaden participation in
education and training opportunities may be
subsumed in this--management's changing perception
of workers, both as employees and as individuals.
As the vice president of a growing electronics
firm commented, "Let's distinguish between what
we'd like to do and the way we'd like to be and
where we are now." As their expectations are
raised, managers are more likely to develop
policies for worker learning and for worktime
flexibility. Only then may the potential gains of
this linkage be realized.

NOTES

1. The Bolivar Project Progress Report February 1978. Prepared by the Harvard University Project on Technology, Work and Character (mimeo), pp. 24-25.

2. See note #I-6, pp. 20, 27.

IV. ISSUES FOR FUTURE POLICY

Designed to test the feasibility of further study, this investigation has, nonetheless, raised several broad policy questions. Employers considering procedures to improve employee productivity and to enhance career opportunities might examine these implications.

Fundamental to these issues is the question of how management will resolve increasing pressure to contain business costs. Will training and education investments be among the first budget items to be severely reduced or eliminated, as is often the case? Might they, instead, be more closely scrutinized for most effective utility? Considering the informality, diversity and private character of employer-sponsored programs, it is not surprising that so little aggregate data exist on the effects of these activities. More unexpected is the frequent lack of consistent data within individual enterprises. If, however, employers are now to make more rational determination of optimum levels and allocations for these investments, they may be prompted to systematize the necessary information.

Such an assessment of the efficacy of training and education would bring into judgment a range of questions now largely ignored. What is or might be the priority of training expenditures when calculated in relation to total labor costs, including, for example, recruitment, turnover and relocation? In terms of total job requirements, might managers wish to determine more exactly the optimum relationship between learning that takes place on and off the job? Beyond equity values, might they also consider whether the concentration at the nonexempt level of training for specific job skills rather than for improvement and enhancement for future duties is, in all instances, the most appropriate for perceived longer range organizational needs. In regard to tuition aid benefits, might policymakers then re-examine the limitation of reimbursement to courses which are immediately job-related? Might some of this assistance be broadened to include a greater range of educational offerings so as to benefit employer as well as employee (as was presumed by the 1978 legislation amending the Internal Revenue Act to cover wider tax deductibility)?

Policymakers may also be moved to question the ways in which better connections with local educational and technical institutions might affect costs, course content and enhanced employee participation in learning. Because some companies already assume a degree of responsibility for other types of personal counseling, might these and other organizations consider the value of a corresponding role for educational advising? Finally, in this review process, might management also become better aware of the degree to which employee participation in nonmandatory education and training may be motivated by other organizational policies--not only those affecting internal mobility, but the less complicated introduction of flexible workhours?

Consideration of new work schedules poses a related set of issues. In evaluating which schedule or combination of schedules will best succeed, management will want to make judgments dependent on the technologies and social characteristics at each enterprise and location. Decisionmakers must take into account the specific problems new time patterns might solve or alleviate, the employee preferences they could meet, and the constraints that need to be overcome--regulations and legislation, and adjustments in supervisory attitudes. They would

be better able then to address the additional
questions that must be answered so that these new
schedules, in addition to other mutual advantages,
might also significantly expand participation in
education and training.

Despite the fact that the effectiveness of
time flexibility in widening employee involvement
relies for greatest efficacy on overall
organizational policies and local conditions,
these patterns can, in fact, offer choices for
learning to nonexempt workers hitherto generally
available only to management. Whereas the shorter
workweek is more narrowly restricted to particular
technologies, flextime is broadly applicable to a
variety of companies. It is also well-suited to
expand both worktime and nonworktime for education
and training. In considering this pattern,
however, employers will need to evaluate which
procedures will best ensure, for example, that
hours are open for on-site activities, rather than
limited to core hours.

The issues arising from utilizing reduced
workhours for learning are more complex because
they involve intrinsic changes in the perception
of part-time employment. Nonetheless, management
might usefully examine the now singular examples
in their several enterprises to determine whether
a wider range of employees, job categories and
levels might prove amenable to part-time
schedules. Part-time employees would thus be more
encouraged to take part in and be better able to
afford education and training at their own
expense. Tuition aid benefits to part-time
employees might also then be more practicably
extended on a wider scale than is now the case.
In this connection, policymakers might find
replicable experience in the long-standing
work-study schemes involving younger adults. And,
looking to the future, leaders in business,

education and government might together examine
the implications of a new form of temporary
worksharing--a combination of part-time work with
education and training.

A final question asks whether employers ought
to look to special programs that concentrate on
making the time-learning connection for women at
lower job levels. Doubtless, the 80 percent of
women still confined to low skilled jobs would
benefit. However, given the danger of further
occupational segregation, such programs might more
profitably be integrated in overall personnel
policies.

Women, as well as men, in lower status jobs
will gain when these policies reflect a broader
vision which would recognize that work and
learning can proceed together; that education
cannot be limited to early years, continuing
education to employees already more "credentialed"
or to the acquisition of narrow skills likely to
obsolesce within the next decade. It would
acknowledge, too, that rigid work schedules--which
restrain continued learning--are not necessarily
equated with efficient job performance.

Might not the price of unrealized
opportunities in individual and organizational
growth prove more costly than those incurred by
the introduction of such related quality-of-
worklife measures?